United States
Department of
Agriculture

Forest
Service

North Central
Research Station

Resource Bulletin
NC-246

Minnesota's Forest Resources in 2003

Patrick D. Miles, Gary J. Brand, and Manfred E. Mielke

North Central Research Station
U.S. Department of Agriculture - Forest Service
1992 Folwell Avenue
Saint Paul, Minnesota 55108
2005
www.ncrs.fs.fed.us

CONTENTS

Minnesota's Forest Resources in 2003

The North Central Research Station's Forest Inventory and Analysis (NCFIA) program began fieldwork for the sixth forest inventory of Minnesota's forest resources in 1999. This inventory initiated the new NCFIA annual inventory system in which one-fifth of the field plots (considered one panel) in the State are measured each year. A complete inventory consists of measuring and compiling the data for all plots (or five panels). Once all panels have been measured, each will be remeasured approximately every 5 years. For example, in Minnesota, the field plots measured in 1999 will be remeasured in 2004.

The fifth and final panel of the sixth inventory of Minnesota's forest resources was completed in 2003. Reports of previous inventories of Minnesota are dated 1936, 1953, 1962, 1977, and 1990. Data presented in this report represent 100 percent of the field plots (or five panels) for a complete inventory and are a combination of the first year's panel from 1999, the second year's panel from 2000, the third year's panel from 2001, the fourth year's panel from 2002, and the fifth year's panel from 2003. Results presented are estimates based on sampling techniques; estimates were compiled assuming the 1999, 2000, 2001, 2002, and 2003 data represent one large sample.

Data from new inventories are often compared with data from earlier inventories to determine trends in forest resources. However, for the comparisons to be valid, the procedures used in the two inventories must be similar. As a result of our ongoing efforts to improve the efficiency and reliability of the inventory, several changes in procedures and definitions have occurred since the last Minnesota inventory in 1990 (Miles *et al.* 1995) (see appendix). These changes may have significant impacts on plot classification variables such as forest type and stand-size class. Some of these changes make it inappropriate to directly compare 2003 data tables with those published for 1990.

RESULTS

Area

The total land area of Minnesota is 50.9 million acres of which 32 percent or 16.2 million acres are forest land (table 1). There are three components to forest land: 1) Timberland[1]— forest land that is not restricted from harvesting by statute, administrative regulation, or designation and is capable of growing trees at a rate of 20 cubic feet per acre per year; 2) Reserved forest land—land that is restricted from harvesting by statute, administrative regulation, or designation (i.e., national parks, wilderness areas, etc.); and 3) Other forest land—low-productivity forest land that is not capable of growing trees at a rate of 20 cubic feet per acre per year.

The estimated area of forest land declined from 16.7 million acres in 1990 to 16.2 million acres in 2003. During the same period, the area of timberland increased slightly from 14.7 million acres in 1990 to

About the Authors:

Patrick D. Miles and **Gary J. Brand** are Research Foresters with the North Central Research Station, St. Paul, MN.

Manfred E. Mielke is a Plant Pathologist with Forest Health Protection, Forest Health Monitoring Program, Northeastern Area State and Private Forestry, St. Paul, MN.

[1] Timberland may not be equivalent to the area actually available for commercial timber harvesting or other access. The actual availability of land for various uses depends upon owner decisions that consider economic, environmental, and social factors.

14.8 million acres in 2003 (fig. 1)[2]. The decrease in forest land and the increase in timberland are due in large part to changes in the reserved and other forest land components. The decline in the area of reserved forest land was due to a change in procedures rather than a change in land use. In 1990 forest plots that were within a reserved boundary were not always visited by field crews. In 2003 all forest plots were visited and a number of plots within the mapped reserved boundaries were determined to be non-reserved. The estimate of reserved forest land decreased from 1,117 thousand acres in 1990 to 942 thousand acres in 2003, and the area estimate of other forest land decreased from 840 thousand acres to 528 thousand acres. Nearly half of this acreage decrease in reserved and other forest land was due to reclassification to non-forest land with the other half due to reclassification to timberland. The net effect was a decrease in the area estimate for forest land and an increase in the area estimate for timberland.

The estimate of forest land in public ownership remained relatively constant over the period (fig. 2). The public timberland estimate, however, increased from 7.6 million acres in 1990 to 8.0 million acres in 2003 with a corresponding decline in the area of other and reserved forest land (table 2).

Private ownership declined from 7.1 million acres to 6.8 million acres over the period. Hardwood forest types are concentrated on private lands (54 percent) while softwood forest types are concentrated on public lands (74 percent).

The aspen/birch forest type, with 6.3 million acres of timberland (table 3), is the dominant forest type in the State (fig. 3) and is an important resource for Minnesota's forest industries. Nearly four-fifths of all the coniferous timberland in the State is in the spruce/fir forest type (3.2 million acres). Between inventories, the estimate of hardwood forest types increased from 10.2 million acres in 1990 to 10.5 million acres in 2003, while the estimate for softwood forest types decreased from 4.4 million acres in 1990 to 4.1 million acres in 2003. This appears to be the result of new stocking and forest typing algorithms used in conjunction with a new plot configuration rather than a

[2] The accuracy bracket atop each bar in figures 1, 5, and 6 provide a measure of reliability of these figures. In 2003 there was a two out of three chance that if a 100-percent inventory had been taken, using the same methods, the result would have been within the limits indicated by the bracket—14,759.8 thousand acres plus or minus 112.2 thousand acres.

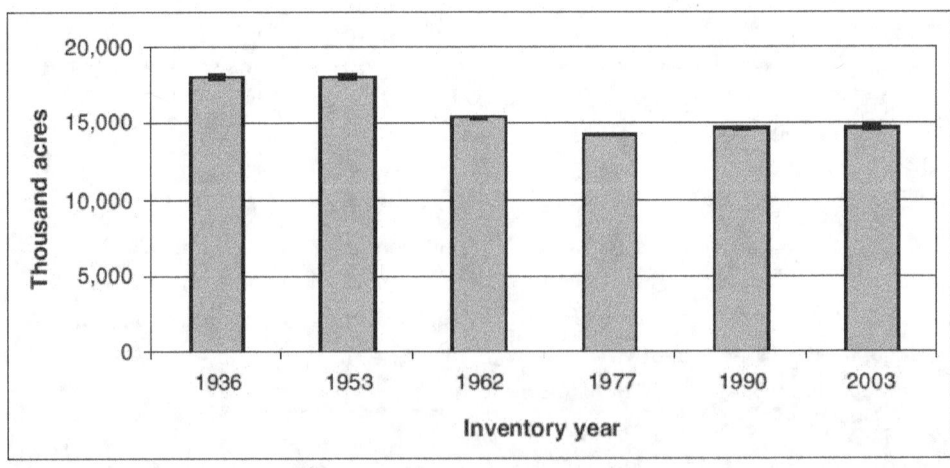

Figure 1.—Area of timberland in Minnesota by inventory year.

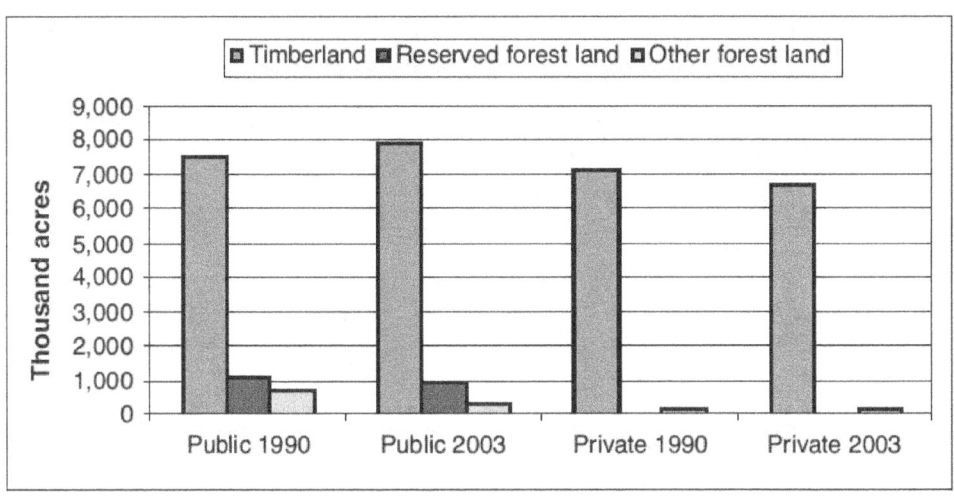

Figure 2.—*Area of forest land in Minnesota by forest land component, owner category, and inventory year.*

change in species composition because roughly 31 percent of the State's growing-stock volume was in softwood tree species in both 1990 and 2003.

The area of timberland by stand-size class showed a consistent trend from 1962 to 1990 (fig. 4). The area of medium stands declined from 8.5 million acres in 1962 to 5.3 million acres in 1990 while the area in large stands increased from 2.4 million to 4.9 million acres.

Changes to the stand-size class algorithm, along with the new plot configuration, make

comparisons of the 2003 stand-size numbers to earlier years difficult at best. From 1990 to 2003 the area classified as medium stands (stands where a plurality of the stocking is in hardwoods 5 to 11 inches d.b.h. and softwoods 5 to 9 inches d.b.h.) rose from 5.3 million to 5.7 million acres, despite a 13-percent decline in the number of poletimber-size trees. Over the same period the area classified as large stands (sawtimber stands where a plurality of the stocking is in trees at least 9 inches d.b.h. for conifers or 11.0 inches d.b.h. for deciduous trees) decreased by 19 percent (947 thousand acres) from 4,890.3 thousand acres

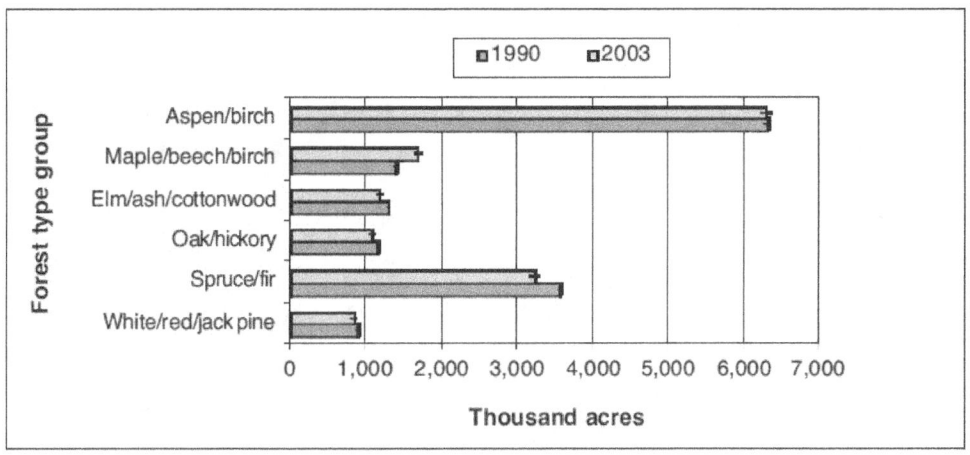

Figure 3.—*Area of timberland in Minnesota in 1990 and 2003 by forest type.*

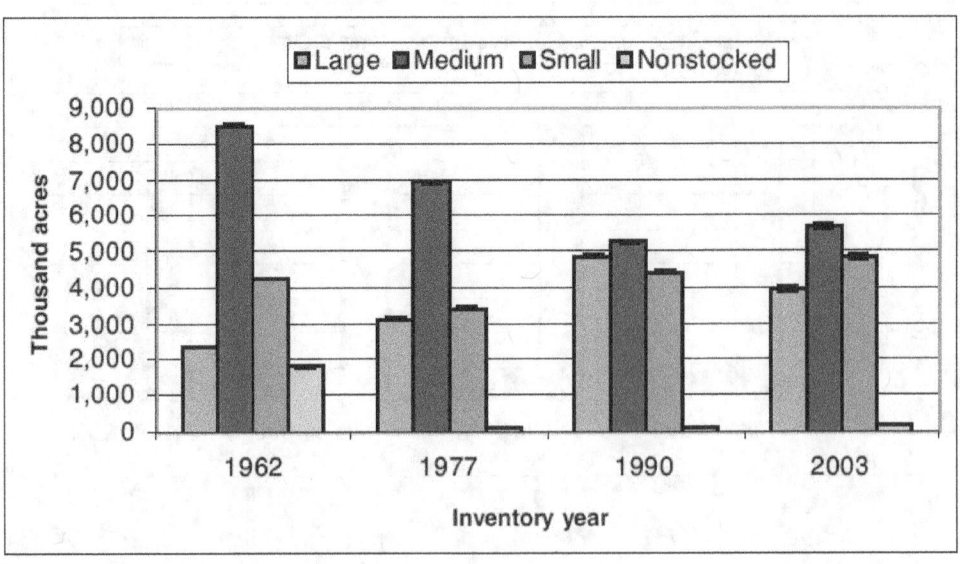

Figure 4.—Area of timberland in Minnesota by stand-size class and inventory year.

to 3,943.4 thousand acres—even though there was only a 4-percent decrease in the number of sawtimber-size trees.

Volume

Historically, volume has been reported as either growing stock or sawtimber. However, there are volumes in noncommercial trees, rough trees, and rotten trees that do not qualify as growing stock but are utilized for wood fiber and fuelwood. Such trees also make important ecological contributions (such as for wildlife habitat, and soil and water protection). With the annualized inventory system and increased

interest in FIA data from an ecological perspective, a greater focus has been placed on all live volume. In 2003, Minnesota had 17.6 billion cubic feet of all live volume on its 16.2 million acres of forest land (table 4). This equates to an average of 1,087 cubic feet of all live volume for each forest land acre in Minnesota.

The net volume of growing stock on timberland in Minnesota was estimated at 15.3 billion cubic feet on 14.8 million acres in 2003 (table 5), or 1,035 cubic feet of growing stock per acre (fig. 5). The 1990 inventory estimates

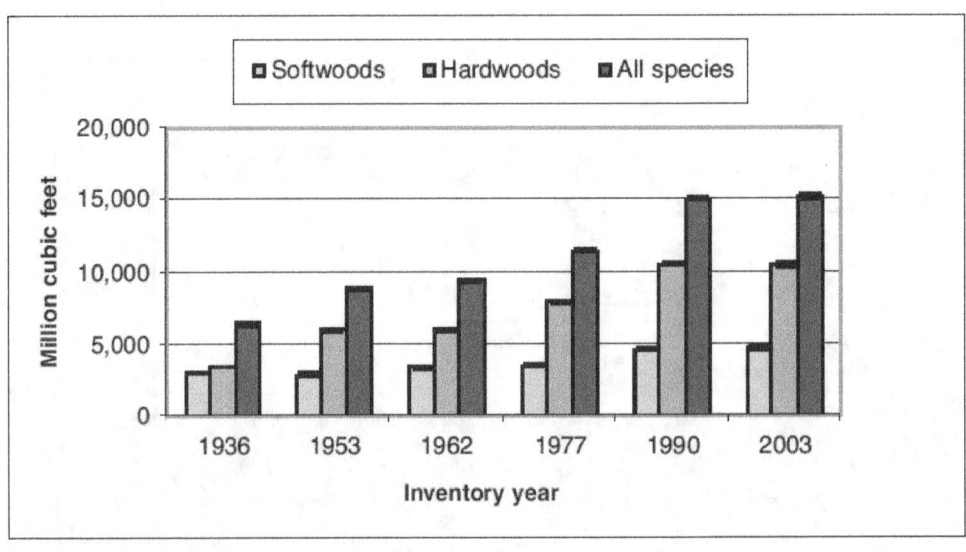

Figure 5.—Growing-stock volume in Minnesota by inventory year.

were 15.1 billion cubic feet of growing stock on 14.7 million acres of timberland, or 1,028 cubic feet of growing stock per acre. While growing-stock volume increased, all live volume on timberland decreased from 17.1 billion cubic feet in 1990 to 16.3 billion cubic feet in 2003 due in part to a decrease in the volume of rough and rotten cull trees from 1.6 billion cubic feet in 1990 to 1.1 billion cubic feet in 2003.

In 2003 hardwoods made up 69 percent of the growing-stock volume and 65 percent of the sawtimber volume in the State (figs. 5 and 6). The cottonwood/aspen species group accounted for 40 percent of the hardwood growing-stock volume, followed by other eastern soft hardwoods (15 percent), ash (11 percent), basswood (8 percent), select white oaks (8 percent), select red oaks (7 percent), soft maple (5 percent), and hard maple (5 percent) (table 6).

Softwood growing-stock volume was estimated at 4.8 billion cubic feet in 2003. The spruce and balsam fir species group accounted for 35 percent of the softwood volume, followed by other eastern softwoods (32 percent), eastern white and red pines (23 percent), and jack pine (9 percent).

The growing-stock volume of poletimber-size trees decreased from 7.8 billion cubic feet in 1990 to 7.2 billion cubic feet in 2003 (table 7) while the growing-stock volume of sawtimber-size trees increased from 7.4 billion cubic feet in 1990 to 8.1 billion cubic feet in 2003 (table 8).

Biomass

Biomass, measured as all live aboveground tree biomass on timberlands, was estimated at 432 million dry tons in 2003 (an average of 29 dry tons per acre) (table 9). Biomass estimates are increasing in importance for analyses on carbon sequestration, wood fiber availability for fuel, and other issues. In 2003, 78 percent of the total biomass was in growing-stock trees, an additional 14 percent was in trees less than 5 inches d.b.h., and the remaining 8 percent was in non-growing-stock trees. Three-quarters of the total biomass was composed of hardwood species. Although total biomass was almost evenly split on private (217 million dry tons) and public (215 million dry tons) timberlands, softwoods made up 35 percent of the total biomass on public lands, but only 15 percent on private lands.

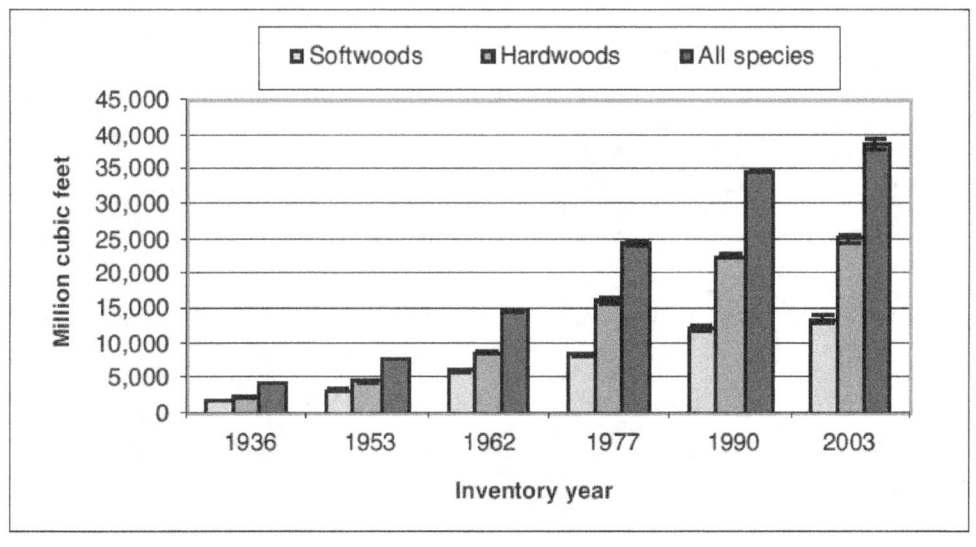

Figure 6.—*Sawtimber volume in Minnesota by inventory year.*

Growth, Removals, and Mortality

The three components of change (growth, removals, and mortality) provide trend information that helps to describe forest changes between inventories.

Net average annual growth between the current and previous inventories is equal to gross growth over the period less mortality over the period divided by the number of growing seasons in the period. The net average annual growth of growing stock on timberland from 1990 to 2003 was 404 million cubic feet (table 10), or approximately 2.6 percent of the current growing-stock inventory on timberland.

Average annual removals of growing stock on timberland from 1990 to 2003 were 249 million cubic feet (table 11), or approximately 1.6 percent of the current growing-stock inventory on timberland. Average annual removals include both trees cut or killed as a result of harvesting (205 million cubic feet) and trees removed from the timberland base as a result of land use change (44 million cubic feet).

Average annual mortality includes trees that died over the period but did not die as a result of timber harvesting (trees that died as a result of timber harvesting are included in removals). Average annual mortality of growing stock on timberland from 1990 to 2003 was 272 million cubic feet (table 12), or approximately 1.8 percent of the current growing-stock inventory on timberland. Average annual mortality is not presented in figure 7 because it has already been removed from gross growth to compute the average net growth number.

Forest Health

The Forest Health Protection staff of the St. Paul Field Officeof the Northeastern Area State and Private Forestry provided the following forest health information.

Insects, pathogens, weather, fire, and other factors cause damage and losses in forests throughout Minnesota every year. Since 1954 the eastern spruce budworm has defoliated spruce/fir forests annually, establishing itself as the most consistent damaging agent in the State. The prevalence of spruce budworm had been declining over most of the past decade, but increased significantly in 2002, then declined again in 2003 by 60 percent to 34,601 acres. In 2003 another defoliator, the forest tent caterpillar, was active on a large scale throughout aspen and birch forests for the fifth consecutive year, although declining to 2.25 million acres, down from 7.4 million acres in 2002. Populations are expected to be much smaller in 2004 with only localized

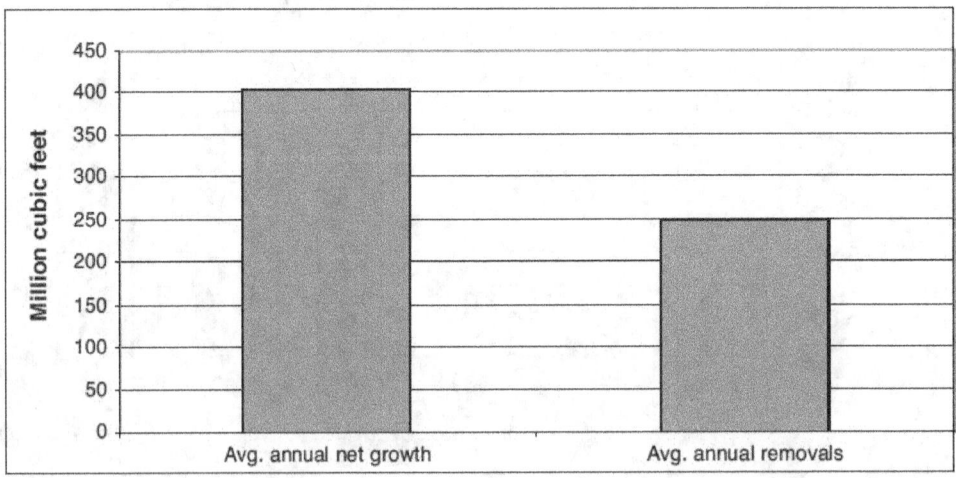

Figure 7.—*Average annual net growth and average annual removals, Minnesota, 1990-2003.*

spots being defoliated. Other significant damage agents active during 2003 were jack pine budworm defoliating 18,546 acres and killing older, open growing jack pine, and the introduced larch casebearer defoliating larch over 1,660 acres, down 40 percent from 2002.

Since 1997, all of these and other defoliating agents have been active, sometimes on some of the same acreages at the same time. Trees that are repeatedly defoliated often sustain measurable growth loss, which, in turn, sometimes results in mortality. Figure 8 shows areas of the State where forested lands have been defoliated between one and six times since 1998.

Mortality from larch beetles declined by 50 percent in 2003 to just over 6,000 acres. Mortality is usually limited to individual trees or small pockets of trees. However, some stands of 30 acres and larger have experienced over 75 percent mortality.

In mid-August of 2002, two-lined chestnut borer damage began to show up in Itasca County. By late August, dieback, topkill, and whole tree mortality were widespread in northern and southern Minnesota. Drought and 2 or more years of forest tent caterpillar defoliation were likely the stress factors contributing to the success of the borers. An aerial survey, flown in September 2003, detected mortality over an additional 12,557 acres in Cass, Itasca, northern Aitkin, northern Crow Wing, and southeastern Baltrami Counties.

Spruce beetle has been killing large diameter white spruce along the Lake Superior shore over the past few years. The amount of mortality is increasing and new infestations continue to be found. The damage is most obvious within a few miles of the lake, but has also been found in Koochiching County as well as in a windbreak in Wadena County.

Oak wilt continues to be one of the greatest concerns in central Minnesota, especially in

Sherburne and Anoka Counties. Following the storms of 1997 and 1998, the number of infection pockets dramatically increased in those areas affected by the storms. As a result, the oak wilt epicenter shifted northwestward into Sherburne County, where storm damage and increased development have put many oaks at risk. An evaluation of ongoing control efforts indicates that some communities are making progress on reducing the number of centers; however, the incidence of oak wilt appears to be increasing overall.

Arguably, agents completely beyond human control, namely the weather, cause the most significant damage. Periods of drought and flooding, snow, ice, cold, and wind damage are an integral component of the State's forest dynamics. In 2003 flooding occurred on almost 8,000 acres, down 30 percent from 2002. Wildfire burned 168 acres, wind/tornado damaged 586 acres and winter injury struck 17 acres. A summary of all damage detected in 2003 is provided in table 13.

For Further Information Contact:
North Central Research Station
USDA Forest Service
1992 Folwell Avenue
St. Paul, MN 55108
or visit our Web site:
www.ncrs.fs.fed.us/4801/.

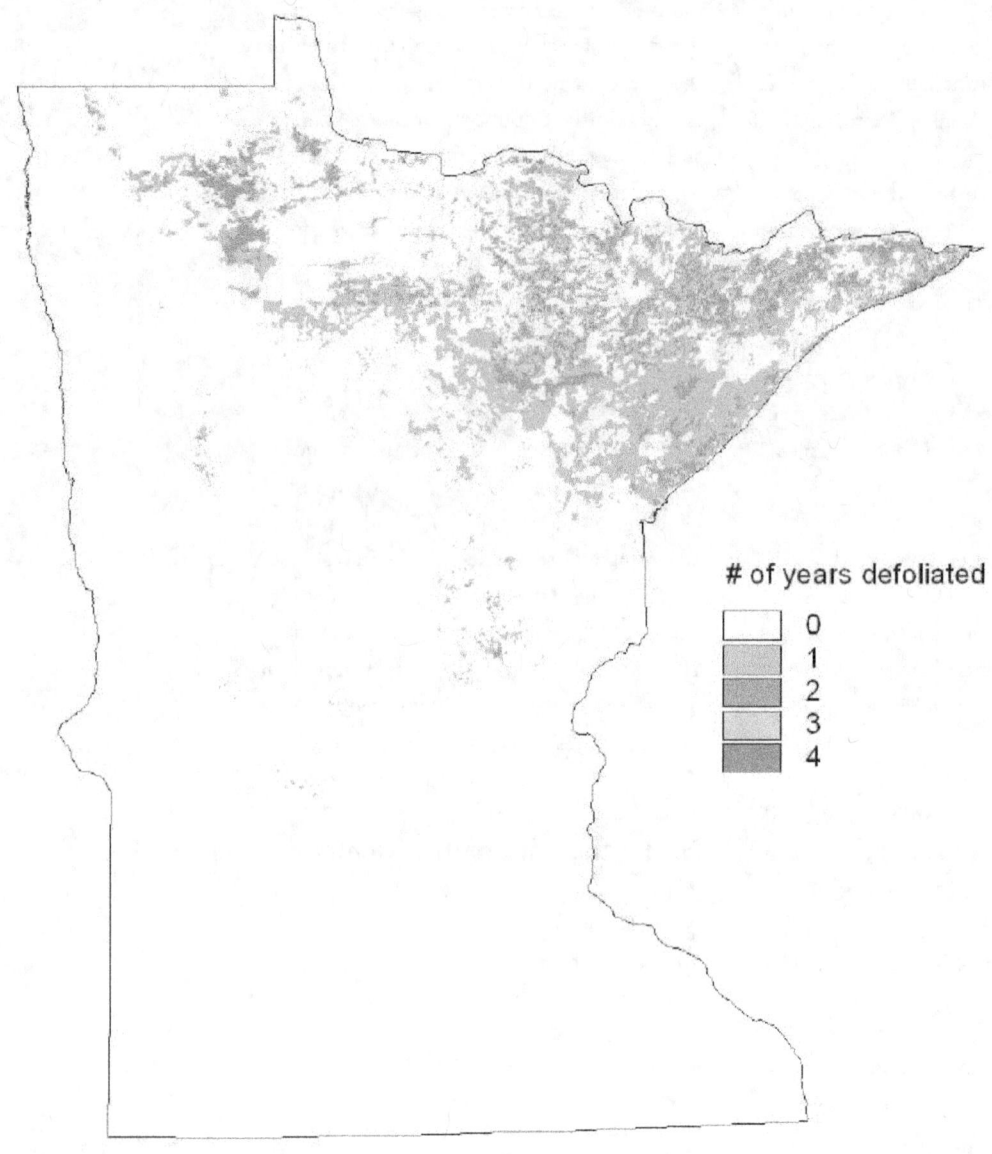

# of years defoliated

0
1
2
3
4

Figure 8.—*Areas with high incidence of defoliation mapped by aerial survey, 1999-2003 (Forest Health Protection, St. Paul Field Office).*

APPENDIX

Inventory Methods

Since the 1990 inventory of Minnesota, several changes have been made in NCFIA inventory methods to improve the quality of the inventory as well as meet increasing demands for timely forest resource information. The most significant difference between inventories is the change from periodic inventories to annual inventories. Historically, NCFIA's periodically inventoried each State on a cycle that averaged about 12 years. However, the need for timely and consistent data across large regions, combined with national legislative mandates, resulted in NCFIA's implementation of an annual inventory system. Minnesota was one of the first States in the North Central region, and one of the first States in the Nation, to be inventoried with this new system, beginning with the 1999 panel of measurements.

With the NCFIA annual inventory system, about one-fifth of all field plots are measured in any one year. After 5 years, an entire inventory cycle will be completed. After the first 5 years, NCFIA will report and analyze results as a moving 5-year average. For example, NCFIA will be able to generate a report based on inventory results for 1999 through 2003 or for 2000 through 2004. Sampling error estimates for the 2003 inventory results are area of forest land, 0.63 percent; area of timberland, 0.76 percent; number of growing-stock trees on timberland, 1.52 percent; volume of growing stock on timberland, 1.42 percent; volume of sawtimber on timberland, 2.02 percent; average annual net growth of growing stock on timberland, 4.34 percent; average annual removals of growing stock on timberland, 5.85 percent; and average annual mortality of growing stock on timberland, 3.40 percent.

Other significant changes between inventories include new remote sensing technology, a new field plot configuration, and additional

remotely sensed and field data. The advent of remote sensing technology since the previous inventory in 1990 has allowed NCFIA to use computer-assisted classifications of Multi-Resolution Land Characterization (MRLC) data and other available remote sensing products to stratify the total area of the State and to improve estimates. Inventories in Minnesota before 1999 used manual interpretation of aerial photos to stratify the sample (1936, 1953, 1962, 1977, and 1990).

New algorithms were used in 1999–2003 to assign forest type and stand-size class to each condition observed on a plot. These algorithms are being used nationwide by FIA to provide consistency among States. The list of recognized forest types, grouping of these forest types for reporting purposes, equations used to assign stocking values to individual trees, definition of nonstocked, and names given to the forest types changed with the new algorithms. As a result, comparisons between the published 1999–2003 measurement results and those published for the 1990 inventory results may not be valid. For additional details on algorithms used in both inventories, please contact NCFIA.

Sampling Phases

The 2003 Minnesota survey was based on a three-phase inventory. The first phase used classified satellite imagery to stratify the State and aerial photographs to select plots for measurement. The second phase measured the traditional FIA suite of mensurational variables, and the third phase focused on a suite of variables related to the health of the forest.

The only land that could not be sampled was (1) private land where field personnel could not obtain permission from the owner to measure the field plot and (2) plots that could not be accessed because of a hazard or danger to field personnel. The methods used in the preparation of this report make the necessary adjustments to account for sites where access was denied or hazardous. There were only 23 denied access or hazardous plots in 1999, 59 in 2000, 66 in 2001, 61 in 2002, and 82 in 2003.

Phase 1

In phase 1 the Minnesota inventory used a computer-assisted classification of satellite imagery. FIA used the classified imagery to form two initial strata—forest and nonforest. Pixels within 60 m (2 pixel widths) of a forest-nonforest boundary formed two additional strata—forest-edge and nonforest-edge. Forest pixels within 60 m on the forest side of a forest-nonforest boundary were classified into forest-edge strata. Pixels within 60 m of the boundary on the nonforest side were classified into nonforest-edge strata. An overlay of all national forest land was used to identify all lands owned by national forests. These national forest lands were treated separately but were also stratified into one of the above four strata. Stratification and estimation were conducted at the State level for national forest lands and at the FIA Inventory unit level for other lands. In the national forest stratum, forest and forest-edge strata were combined.

Phase 2

Phase 2 of the inventory consisted of the measurement of the annual sample of field plots in Minnesota. Current FIA precision standards for annual inventories require a sampling intensity of one plot for approximately every 6,000 acres. FIA has established a grid that divides the entire area of the United States into non-overlapping hexagons, each of which contains approximately 5,937 acres (McRoberts 1999). A grid of field plots was established by selecting one plot from each hexagon based on the following rules: (1) if a Forest Health Monitoring (FHM) plot (Mangold 1998) fell within a hexagon, it was selected as the grid plot; (2) if no FHM plot fell within a hexagon, the existing NCFIA plot from the 1990 inventory nearest the hexagon center was selected as the grid plot; and (3) if neither FHM nor existing NCFIA plots fell within the hexagon, a new NCFIA plot was established in the hexagon (McRoberts 1999). This grid of plots is designated the Federal base sample and is considered an equal probability sample; its measurement in Minnesota is funded by the Federal government.

The total Federal base sample was systematically divided into five interpenetrating, non-overlapping subsamples or panels. Each year the plots in a single panel are measured, and panels are selected on a 5-year, rotating basis (McRoberts 1999). For estimation purposes, the measurement of each panel of plots may be considered an independent systematic sample of all land in a State. Field crews measure vegetation on plots forested at the time of the last inventory and on plots currently classified as forest by trained photointerpreters using aerial photos or digital orthoquads.

Phase 3

NCFIA has two categories of field plot measurements—phase 2 field plots and phase 3 plots (FHM plots)—to optimize our ability to collect data when available for measurement. Both types of plot are systematically distributed both geographically and temporally. Phase 3 plots are measured with the full suite of FHM vegetative and health variables collected as well as the full suite of measures associated with phase 2 plots. Phase 3 plots must be measured between June 1 and August 30 to accommodate the additional measurement of nonwoody understory vegetation, ground cover, soils, and other variables. The complete 5-year annual inventory includes 643 phase 3 plots of which 267 are forested. On the remaining plots, referred to as phase 2 plots, only variables that can be measured throughout the entire year are collected. In Minnesota, the complete 5-year annual inventory includes 5,165 phase 2 forested plots. The 1999–2003 annual inventory results represent field measures on 4,782 timberland, 383 other forest land, and 11,259 nonforest land plots. The above number of field plots represents a single intensification for the standard base Federal sample in 1999 and a double intensification for 2000, 2001, 2002, and 2003. This double intensification was made possible by additional resources provided by the State of Minnesota.

The new national FIA 4-point cluster plot configuration (fig. 9) was used for data collection during the 1999–2003 measurements of Minnesota. The national plot configuration requires mapping forest conditions on each plot.

The overall plot layout for the new configuration consists of four subplots. The centers of subplots 2, 3, and 4 are located 120 feet from the center of subplot 1. The azimuths to subplots 2, 3, and 4 are 0, 120, and 240 degrees, respectively. The center of the new plot is located at the same point as the center of the previous plot if a previous plot existed within the sample unit. Trees with a d.b.h. of 5 inches and larger are measured on a 24-foot-radius (1/24 acre) circular subplot. All trees less than 5 inches d.b.h. are measured on a 6.8-foot-radius (1/300 acre) circular microplot located 12 feet east of the center of each of the four subplots. Forest conditions that occur on any of the four subplots are recorded. Factors that differentiate forest conditions are changes in forest type, stand-size class, land use, ownership, and density. Each condition that occurs anywhere on any of the subplots is identified, described, and mapped

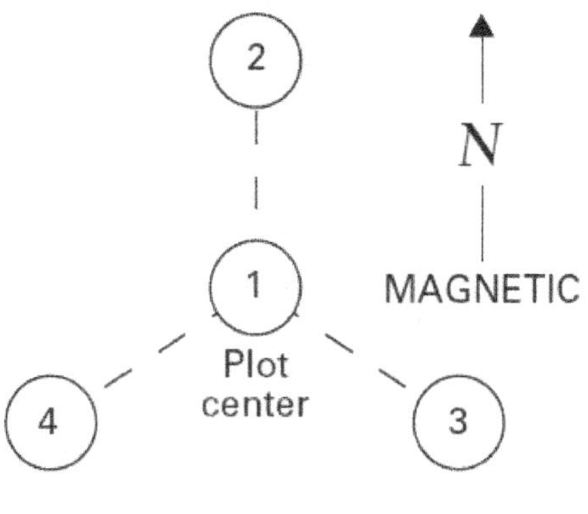

if the area of the condition meets or exceeds 1 acre in size and 120 feet in width. Field plot measurements are combined with phase 1 estimates in the compilation process and table production. The number of tables generated from less than five panels of data is limited. However, as additional annual inventories are completed, the number of tables will increase until year 5, when all statewide inventory summary tables will be available in both printed and electronic formats. For additional information, contact:

Program Manager
Forest Inventory and Analysis
North Central Research Station
1992 Folwell Ave.
St. Paul, MN 55108

Or

State Forester
Division of Forestry
Minnesota Department of Natural Resources
P.O. Box 44, 500 Lafayette Road
St. Paul, MN 55155

LITERATURE CITED

Mangold, R.D. 1998.
Forest health monitoring field methods guide (National 1998). Research Triangle Park, NC: U.S. Department of Agriculture, Forest Service, National Forest Health Monitoring Program. 429 p. (Revision 0, April 1998).

McRoberts, R.E. 1999
Joint annual forest inventory and monitoring system, the North Central perspective. Journal of Forestry. 97(12): 27-31.

Miles, P.D.; Chen, C.M.; Leatherberry, E.C. 1995.
Minnesota forest statistics, 1990, revised. Resour. Bull. NC-158. St. Paul, MN: U.S. Department of Agriculture, Forest Service, North Central Forest Experiment Station. 139 p.

Figure 13. — Current NCFIA field plot design.

TABLE TITLES

Table 1.—*Area of forest land by forest type group, forest type, and owner category, Minnesota, 1999–2003*

Table 2.—*Area of timberland by major forest type group, stand origin, and owner category, Minnesota, 1999–2003*

Table 3.—*Area of timberland by forest type group, forest type, and stand-size class, Minnesota, 1999–2003*

Table 4.—*Net volume of all live trees on forest land by species group, species, and owner category, Minnesota, 1999–2003*

Table 5.—*Net volume of all live trees and salvable dead trees on timberland by class of timber and softwood/hardwood species category, Minnesota, 1999–2003*

Table 6.—*Net volume of growing stock on timberland by forest group, forest type, and softwood/hardwood species category, Minnesota, 1999–2003*

Table 7.—*Net volume of growing stock on timberland by species group, species, and diameter class, Minnesota, 1999–2003*

Table 8.—*Net volume of sawtimber on timberland by species group, species, and diameter class, Minnesota, 1999–2003*

Table 9.—*All live aboveground tree biomass on timberland by owner category, softwood/hardwood species category, and tree component, Minnesota, 1999–2003*

Table 10.—*Average annual net growth of growing stock on timberland by species group and owner category, Minnesota, 1990 to 1999–2003*

Table 11.—*Average annual removals of growing stock on timberland by species group and owner category, Minnesota, 1990 to 1999–2003*

Table 12.—*Average annual mortality of growing stock on timberland by species group and owner category, Minnesota, 1990 to 1999–2003*

Table 13.—*Detection survey results, Minnesota, 2003 (Forest Health Protection, Saint Paul Field Office)*

TABLES

Table 1. — Area of forest land by forest type group, forest type, and
owner category. Minnesota, 1999-2003

(In thousand acres)

| Forest type group/ forest type | All owners | Owner category | | |
		Public	Private	Unidentified owner
Softwood type groups				
White / red / jack pine group				
Jack pine	481.8	325.2	156.5	--
Red pine	406.0	264.6	141.3	--
Eastern white pine	116.1	84.1	32.0	--
All forest types	1,003.8	674.0	329.9	--
Spruce / fir group				
Balsam fir	447.7	281.0	166.6	--
White spruce	112.4	77.9	34.4	--
Black spruce	1,620.1	1,353.7	266.5	--
Tamarack	891.9	726.0	165.9	--
Northern white-cedar	624.9	503.4	121.5	--
All forest types	3,697.0	2,942.0	755.0	--
Pinyon / juniper group				
Eastern redcedar	16.9	2.7	14.2	--
All forest types	16.9	2.7	14.2	--
Exotic softwoods group				
Scotch pine	3.9	--	3.9	--
All forest types	3.9	--	3.9	--
All softwood groups	4,721.7	3,618.7	1,103.0	--
Hardwood type groups				
Oak / pine group				
White pine / red oak / white ash	86.1	39.7	46.5	--
Eastern redcedar / hardwood	8.5	--	8.5	--
Other pine / hardwood	192.4	100.1	92.3	--
All forest types	287.1	139.8	147.3	--
Oak / hickory group				
Oak / hickory group	1.5	0.5	1.0	--
Post oak / blackjack oak	65.8	9.6	56.2	--
White oak / red oak / hickory	251.7	39.3	212.5	--
White oak	14.0	2.8	11.3	--
Northern red oak	305.1	91.2	213.9	--
Bur oak	202.0	26.7	175.3	--
Black walnut	7.3	--	7.3	--
Red maple / oak	39.6	12.3	27.3	--
Mixed upland hardwoods	275.1	34.6	240.4	--
All forest types	1,162.3	217.0	945.3	--

(Table 1 continued on next page)

14

(Table 1 continued)

Forest type group/ forest type	Owner category			
	All owners	Public	Private	Unidentified owner
Hardwood type groups				
Elm / ash / cottonwood group				
Elm / ash / cottonwood group	2.9	0.7	2.2	--
Black ash / American elm / red maple	886.3	433.2	453.1	--
River birch / sycamore	24.6	21.3	3.3	--
Cottonwood	40.4	15.9	24.5	--
Willow	49.4	16.8	32.7	--
Sycamore / pecan / American elm	8.0	4.0	4.0	--
Sugarberry / hackberry / elm / green ash	205.7	26.3	179.4	--
Silver maple / American elm	40.8	10.0	30.8	--
Red maple / lowland	15.8	5.0	10.8	--
Cottonwood / willow	10.3	4.2	6.2	--
All forest types	1,284.2	537.4	746.8	--
Maple / beech / birch group				
Maple / beech / birch group	0.2	0.2	--	--
Sugar maple / beech / yellow birch	593.0	272.4	320.6	--
Black cherry	5.4	--	5.4	--
Cherry / ash / yellow-poplar	6.0	--	6.0	--
Hard maple / basswood	909.2	331.7	577.5	--
Elm / ash / locust	147.6	30.1	117.5	--
Red maple / upland	96.2	45.7	50.5	--
All forest types	1,757.6	680.0	1,077.6	--
Aspen / birch group				
Aspen / birch group	4.5	2.4	2.1	--
Aspen	5,109.6	2,850.8	2,258.8	--
Paper birch	1,207.4	814.5	392.9	--
Balsam poplar	460.5	233.5	226.9	--
All forest types	6,782.0	3,901.3	2,880.7	--
Exotic hardwoods group				
Other exotic hardwoods	3.8	--	3.8	--
All forest types	3.8	--	3.8	--
All hardwood groups	11,277.0	5,475.4	5,801.6	--
Nonstocked	231.7	138.2	93.4	--
All forest groups	16,230.3	9,232.4	6,998.0	--

All table cells without observations in the inventory sample are indicated by --. Table value of 0.0 indicates the acres round to less than 0.1 thousand acres. Columns and rows may not add to their totals due to rounding.

15

Table 2. -- Area of timberland by major forest type group,
stand origin, and owner category, Minnesota, 1999-2003

(In thousand acres)

Major forest type group and stand origin	All owners	Owner category		
		Public	Private	Unidentified owner
Softwood type groups				
Natural	3,628.8	2,751.1	877.7	--
Planted	446.0	278.4	167.6	--
All softwood types	4,074.8	3,029.5	1,045.3	--
Hardwood type groups				
Natural	10,299.3	4,735.5	5,563.7	--
Planted	181.0	90.3	90.6	--
All hardwood types	10,480.2	4,825.9	5,654.4	--
Nonstocked	204.8	117.9	86.9	--
All groups	14,759.8	7,973.2	6,786.6	--

All table cells without observations in the inventory sample are indicated by --. Table
value of 0.0 indicates the acres round to less than 0.1 thousand acres. Columns and
rows may not add to their totals due to rounding.

(Tables continued on next page)

Table 3. -- Area of timberland by forest type group, forest type, and stand-size class, Minnesota, 1999-2003

(In thousand acres)

Forest type group/ forest type	All stands	Stand-size class			
		Sawtimber	Poletimber	Sapling-seedling	Non-stocked
Softwood type groups					
White / red / jack pine group					
Jack pine	387.9	160.9	157.8	69.2	--
Red pine	373.9	164.3	136.7	72.9	--
Eastern white pine	75.0	59.1	8.9	7.0	--
All forest types	836.8	384.3	303.3	149.1	--
Spruce / fir group					
Balsam fir	374.5	60.9	125.0	188.7	--
White spruce	93.0	11.3	34.5	47.3	--
Black spruce	1,355.1	23.6	408.5	923.0	--
Tamarack	821.8	75.9	324.8	421.1	--
Northern white-cedar	573.5	251.9	260.0	61.6	--
All forest types	3,218.0	423.6	1,152.7	1,641.6	--
Pinyon / juniper group					
Eastern redcedar	16.9	6.9	--	10.0	--
All forest types	16.9	6.9	--	10.0	--
Exotic softwoods group					
Scotch pine	3.1	1.4	1.6	--	--
All forest types	3.1	1.4	1.6	--	--
All softwood groups	4,074.8	816.3	1,457.7	1,800.8	--
Hardwood type groups					
Oak / pine group					
White pine / red oak / white ash	64.9	33.8	18.4	12.7	--
Eastern redcedar / hardwood	5.9	--	5.0	0.9	--
Other pine / hardwood	169.2	79.1	55.5	34.7	--
All forest types	240.1	112.9	78.9	48.3	--
Oak / hickory group					
Oak / hickory group	1.5	0.6	0.9	--	--
Post oak / blackjack oak	62.9	36.5	11.7	14.7	--
White oak / red oak / hickory	242.6	152.7	77.9	11.9	--
White oak	14.0	11.3	2.8	--	--
Northern red oak	281.5	200.5	70.8	10.2	--
Bur oak	161.9	117.8	35.2	8.9	--
Black walnut	7.3	6.4	0.9	--	--
Red maple / oak	39.6	2.3	19.9	17.4	--
Mixed upland hardwoods	267.6	120.3	108.4	38.9	--
All forest types	1,079.0	648.4	328.6	102.0	--
Elm / ash / cottonwood group					
Elm / ash / cottonwood group	2.9	0.8	2.1	--	--
Black ash / American elm / red maple	802.7	123.8	455.0	223.9	--
River birch / sycamore	24.6	3.3	0.8	20.5	--
Cottonwood	38.5	38.3	0.2	--	--
Willow	42.4	6.1	2.2	34.2	--
Sycamore / pecan / American elm	8.0	4.2	--	3.9	--
Sugarberry / hackberry / elm / green ash	195.8	80.8	84.4	30.7	--
Silver maple / American elm	37.4	34.2	3.2	--	--
Red maple / lowland	15.8	6.1	0.8	8.9	--
Cottonwood / willow	10.3	0.4	--	0.9	--
All forest types	1,178.4	306.9	548.6	322.9	--

(Table 3 continued on next page)

(Table 3 continued)

Forest type group/ forest type	All stands	Stand-size class		
		Sawtimber	Poletimber	Sapling-seedling	Non-stocked

Forest type group/ forest type	All stands	Sawtimber	Poletimber	Sapling-seedling	Non-stocked
Hardwood type groups					
Maple / beech / birch group					
Maple / beech / birch group	0.2	--	0.2	--	--
Sugar maple / beech / yellow birch	555.4	222.0	269.5	63.8	--
Black cherry	5.4	--	--	5.4	--
Cherry / ash / yellow-poplar	6.0	2.7	--	3.3	--
Hard maple / basswood	879.5	563.2	295.0	21.2	--
Elm / ash / locust	139.0	58.8	57.7	22.6	--
Red maple / upland	96.2	15.2	55.9	25.1	--
All forest types	1,681.7	862.0	678.4	141.3	--
Aspen / birch group					
Aspen / birch group	4.5	1.1	2.7	0.8	--
Aspen	4,825.5	943.5	1,765.6	2,116.4	--
Paper birch	1,021.2	216.6	623.1	181.5	--
Balsam poplar	446.0	73.7	229.7	142.7	--
All forest types	6,297.2	1,234.8	2,621.0	2,441.4	--
Exotic hardwoods group					
Other exotic hardwoods	3.8	2.2	1.7	--	--
All forest types	3.8	2.2	1.7	--	--
All hardwood groups	10,480.2	3,167.1	4,257.2	3,056.0	--
Nonstocked	204.8	--	--	--	204.8
All forest groups	14,759.8	3,963.4	5,714.9	4,856.7	204.8

All table cells without observations in the inventory sample are indicated by -- Table value of 0.0 indicates the acres round to less than 0.1 thousand acres. Columns and rows may not add to their totals due to rounding.

Table 4. — Net volume of all live trees on forest land by species group, species, and owner category, Minnesota, 1999-2003

(In thousand cubic feet)

Species group/ species	All owners	Owner category		
		Public	Private	Unidentified owner
Softwoods				
Other yellow pines				
Scotch pine	3,945	- -	3,945	- -
All species	3,945	- -	3,945	- -
Eastern white and red pines				
Red pine	837,156	572,447	264,709	- -
Eastern white pine	450,276	303,912	146,364	- -
All species	1,287,431	876,358	411,073	- -
Jack pine				
Jack pine	540,910	368,705	172,205	- -
All species	540,910	368,705	172,205	- -
Spruce and balsam fir				
Balsam fir	690,816	417,930	272,887	- -
White spruce	296,573	207,406	89,167	- -
Black spruce	914,801	740,933	173,868	- -
All species	1,902,191	1,366,269	535,922	- -
Other eastern softwoods				
Eastern redcedar	19,397	607	18,790	- -
Larch spp.	298	186	113	- -
Tamarack (native)	661,690	464,751	196,938	- -
Blue spruce	45	- -	45	- -
Austrian pine	1,249	- -	1,249	- -
Northern white-cedar	1,015,568	766,732	248,837	- -
All species	1,698,248	1,232,276	465,972	- -
Total softwoods	5,432,725	3,843,608	1,589,117	- -
Hardwoods				
Select white oaks				
White oak	113,917	23,887	90,030	- -
Swamp white oak	8,379	6,772	1,607	- -
Bur oak	872,895	169,340	703,554	- -
All species	995,191	200,000	795,191	- -
Select red oaks				
Northern red oak	883,010	311,152	571,859	- -
All species	883,010	311,152	571,859	- -
Other red oaks				
Northern pin oak	85,689	8,597	77,092	- -
Black oak	5,552	1,597	3,955	- -
All species	91,241	10,194	81,047	- -
Hickory				
Hickory spp.	51	- -	51	- -
Bitternut hickory	10,158	85	10,073	- -
Shagbark hickory	18,509	1,082	17,428	- -
All species	28,719	1,167	27,552	- -
Yellow birch				
Yellow birch	53,542	35,580	17,962	- -
All species	53,542	35,580	17,962	- -

(Table 4 continued on next page)

20

(Table 4 continued)

Species group/ species	Owner category			
	All owners	Public	Private	Unidentified owner
Hardwoods				
Hard maple				
Sugar maple	679,339	333,508	345,831	--
All species	679,339	333,508	345,831	--
Soft maple				
Red maple	529,959	261,866	268,093	--
Silver maple	165,434	58,079	107,354	--
All species	695,393	319,946	375,447	--
Ash				
White ash	4,806	769	4,037	--
Black ash	891,126	433,210	457,915	--
Green ash	338,979	73,260	265,719	--
All species	1,234,910	507,239	727,671	--
Cottonwood and aspen				
Cottonwood and poplar spp	493	--	493	--
Balsam poplar	472,921	259,033	213,888	--
Eastern cottonwood	126,552	62,925	63,628	--
Bigtooth aspen	368,914	162,840	206,075	--
Quaking aspen	3,738,077	2,099,461	1,638,616	--
All species	4,706,957	2,584,258	2,122,699	--
Basswood				
American basswood	905,199	302,609	602,591	--
All species	905,199	302,609	602,591	--
Black walnut				
Black walnut	31,358	3,946	27,413	--
All species	31,358	3,946	27,413	--
Other eastern soft hardwoods				
Boxelder	128,057	12,355	115,702	--
Paper birch	1,389,666	889,093	500,573	--
Hackberry	17,892	1,683	16,209	--
Butternut	15,831	4,095	11,736	--
Black cherry	30,856	4,792	26,065	--
Black willow	38,238	11,618	26,620	--
White willow	186	186	--	--
Elm spp.	48	48	--	--
American elm	186,216	40,437	145,779	--
Siberian elm	4,377	64	4,313	--
Slippery elm	38,434	2,269	36,165	--
All species	1,849,801	966,640	883,161	--
Other eastern hard hardwoods				
Sweet birch	352	--	352	--
Honeylocust	273	--	273	--
Red mulberry	80	47	33	--
Black locust	4,460	--	4,460	--
Rock elm	6,909	1,141	5,768	--
All species	12,073	1,188	10,886	--

(Table 4 continued on next page)

(Table 4 continued)

Species group/ species	Owner category			
	All owners	Public	Private	Unidentified owner
Hardwoods				
Eastern noncommercial hardwoods				
Mountain maple	183	152	31	--
Serviceberry spp.	--	--	--	--
American hornbeam, musclewood	1,550	671	879	--
Hawthorn spp.	1,991	--	1,991	--
Apple spp.	369	--	369	--
Eastern hophornbeam	27,146	3,434	23,712	--
Cherry and plum spp.	--	--	--	--
Pin cherry	434	291	143	--
Chokecherry	970	726	244	--
Canada plum	--	--	--	--
American plum	430	77	353	--
Willow spp.	5,227	867	4,360	--
Peachleaf willow	3,604	1,090	2,513	--
American mountain-ash	678	576	102	--
Other or unknown tree	587	--	587	--
All species	43,169	7,885	35,284	--
Total hardwoods	12,209,903	5,585,309	6,624,594	--
All species groups	17,642,628	9,428,918	8,213,710	--

All table cells without observations in the inventory sample are indicated by --. Table value of 0 indicates that the volume rounds to less than 1 thousand cubic feet. Columns and rows may not add to their totals due to rounding.

Table 5. -- Net volume of all live trees and salvable dead trees on timberland
by class of timber and softwood/hardwood species category, Minnesota, 1999-2003

(In thousand cubic feet)

Class of timber	All species	Softwood species	Hardwood species
Live trees			
Growing-stock trees			
Sawtimber			
Saw log portion	6,286,689	2,289,019	3,997,669
Upper stem portion	1,807,786	313,013	1,494,774
Total	8,094,475	2,602,032	5,492,443
Poletimber	7,178,274	2,154,664	5,023,610
All growing-stock trees	15,272,749	4,756,696	10,516,053
Cull trees			
Rough trees[1]			
Sawtimber size	691,266	65,647	625,619
Poletimber size	211,858	25,586	186,272
Total	903,124	91,233	811,892
Rotten trees[1]			
Sawtimber size	133,377	21,053	112,324
Poletimber size	27,913	4,411	23,503
Total	161,290	25,463	135,827
All live cull trees	1,064,415	116,696	947,719
All live trees	16,337,163	4,873,392	11,463,772
Salvable dead trees			
Sawtimber size	141,179	53,857	87,322
Poletimber size	134,366	57,505	76,861
All salvable dead trees	275,545	111,362	164,183
All classes	16,612,708	4,984,754	11,627,954

All table cells without observations in the inventory sample are indicated by -- Table value of 0 indicates
that the volume rounds to less than 1 thousand cubic feet. Columns and rows may not add to their totals
due to rounding.
[1] Includes noncommercial species.

Table 6. – Net volume of growing stock on timberland by forest type group, forest type, and softwood/hardwood species category, Minnesota, 1999-2003

(In thousand cubic feet)

Forest type group/ forest type	All species	Softwood species	Hardwood species
Softwood type groups			
White / red / jack pine group			
Jack pine	432,736	376,580	56,156
Red pine	709,468	665,700	43,768
Eastern white pine	160,062	146,839	13,223
All forest types	1,302,266	1,189,119	113,147
Spruce / fir group			
Balsam fir	299,705	215,415	84,290
White spruce	73,150	61,811	11,338
Black spruce	705,650	673,512	32,138
Tamarack	516,438	506,096	10,342
Northern white-cedar	886,660	799,389	87,271
All forest types	2,481,603	2,256,224	225,379
Pinyon / juniper group			
Eastern redcedar	8,354	6,518	1,836
All forest types	8,354	6,518	1,836
Exotic softwoods group			
Scotch pine	3,200	3,123	77
All forest types	3,200	3,123	77
All softwood groups	3,795,423	3,454,984	340,439
Hardwood type groups			
Oak / pine group			
White pine / red oak / white ash	125,008	76,851	48,157
Eastern redcedar / hardwood	2,715	2,027	688
Other pine / hardwood	197,500	111,151	86,349
All forest types	325,223	190,028	135,195
Oak / hickory group			
Oak / hickory group	92	- -	92
Post oak / blackjack oak	75,042	1,489	73,554
White oak / red oak / hickory	318,162	6,272	311,890
White oak	20,097	- -	20,097
Northern red oak	466,964	2,268	464,695
Bur oak	245,952	2,048	243,903
Black walnut	8,065	- -	8,065
Red maple / oak	26,057	1,292	24,765
Mixed upland hardwoods	297,662	9,133	288,530
All forest types	1,458,092	22,502	1,435,590

(Table 6 continued on next page)

(Table 6 continued)

Forest type group/ forest type	All species	Softwood species	Hardwood species
Hardwood type groups			
Elm / ash / cottonwood group			
Elm / ash / cottonwood group	1,881	- -	1,881
Black ash / American elm / red maple	812,532	102,418	710,115
River birch / sycamore	7,335	2,133	5,202
Cottonwood	117,428	- -	117,428
Willow	16,510	1,326	15,184
Sycamore / pecan / American elm	2,042	1,199	844
Sugarberry / hackberry / elm / green ash	193,991	5,413	188,578
Silver maple / American elm	98,260	- -	98,260
Red maple / lowland	5,511	3,007	2,504
Cottonwood / willow	22,249	573	21,676
All forest types	1,277,740	116,068	1,161,672
Maple / beech / birch group			
Sugar maple / beech / yellow birch	696,214	56,402	639,812
Black cherry	1,227	- -	1,227
Cherry / ash / yellow-poplar	3,237	1,159	2,079
Hard maple / basswood	1,531,523	38,605	1,492,919
Elm / ash / locust	152,939	3,927	149,012
Red maple / upland	81,032	11,447	69,585
All forest types	2,466,172	111,539	2,354,633
Aspen / birch group			
Aspen / birch group	4,328	458	3,870
Aspen	4,409,824	534,744	3,875,080
Paper birch	1,145,436	265,992	879,444
Balsam poplar	377,901	53,964	323,937
All forest types	5,937,489	855,158	5,082,331
Exotic hardwoods group			
Other exotic hardwoods	3,180	- -	3,180
All forest types	3,180	- -	3,180
All hardwood groups	11,467,897	1,295,296	10,172,601
Nonstocked	9,428	6,416	3,013
All forest groups	15,272,749	4,756,696	10,516,053

All table cells without observations in the inventory sample are indicated by --. Table value of 0.0 indicates the acres round to less than 0.1 thousand acres. Columns and rows may not add to their totals due to rounding.

Table 7 – Net volume of growing stock on timberland by species group, species, and diameter class, Minnesota, 1999-2003

(In thousand cubic feet)

Species group/ species	All classes	Diameter class (inches at breast height)									
		5.0-6.9	7.0-8.9	9.0-10.9	11.0-12.9	13.0-14.9	15.0-16.9	17.0-18.9	19.0-20.9	21.0-28.9	29.0+
Softwoods											
Other yellow pines											
Scotch pine	3,204	449	790	1,076	888	--	--	--	--	--	--
All species	3,204	449	790	1,076	888	--	--	--	--	--	--
Eastern white and red pines											
Red pine	770,765	73,673	126,997	127,590	91,565	87,386	70,176	62,584	66,545	62,598	2,680
Eastern white pine	334,641	7,656	18,115	19,304	28,344	27,507	34,413	40,532	43,715	86,846	79,209
All species	1,105,405	81,328	145,112	146,895	119,910	114,893	104,589	103,086	109,260	149,444	30,890
Jack pine											
Jack pine	431,310	57,484	93,736	109,227	82,420	52,946	23,169	8,014	4,315	--	--
All species	431,310	57,484	93,736	109,227	82,420	52,946	23,169	8,014	4,315	--	--
Spruce and balsam fir											
Balsam fir	646,094	190,168	207,476	132,871	69,191	33,420	11,245	740	974	--	--
White spruce	264,957	30,007	47,030	49,015	41,270	27,473	29,312	18,894	7,654	14,301	--
Black spruce	776,263	365,633	247,887	113,046	35,245	9,883	3,726	1,074	--	--	--
All species	1,687,313	585,578	502,393	294,932	145,705	70,785	44,282	20,709	8,626	14,301	--
Other eastern softwoods											
Eastern redcedar	16,400	3,654	3,354	4,325	3,269	1,797	--	--	--	--	--
Larch spp.	146	34	113	--	--	--	--	--	--	--	--
Tamarack (native)	633,329	184,205	185,571	126,825	71,773	32,184	16,050	9,864	2,326	4,531	--
Blue spruce	45	45	--	--	--	--	--	--	--	--	--
Austrian pine	761	48	261	182	270	--	--	--	--	--	--
Northern white-cedar	878,762	125,372	185,136	167,743	140,363	114,944	60,003	40,062	18,737	26,401	--
All species	1,529,463	313,358	374,435	298,075	215,675	148,925	76,053	49,946	21,063	30,932	--
Total softwoods											
All species	4,756,696	1,038,196	1,116,466	651,206	564,599	387,549	248,692	181,755	143,266	194,677	30,890
Hardwoods											
Select white oaks											
White oak	91,213	2,735	5,026	6,235	13,465	14,462	11,388	9,245	6,688	15,419	4,549
Swamp white oak	8,379	37	--	--	--	--	609	--	2,302	--	5,431
Bur oak	717,263	54,348	83,636	107,723	99,160	85,329	72,508	68,197	38,050	92,374	16,919
All species	816,875	57,120	88,662	115,959	112,625	99,791	84,504	77,442	47,060	107,794	25,899
Select red oaks											
Northern red oak	783,843	21,547	54,300	93,455	115,338	134,790	101,560	78,955	62,347	96,220	25,333
All species	783,843	21,547	54,360	93,455	115,336	134,790	101,560	78,955	62,347	96,220	25,333
Other red oaks											
Northern pin oak	63,970	1,470	3,423	3,146	7,317	7,410	9,265	15,639	5,970	10,330	--
Black oak	3,718	--	--	158	253	398	--	641	--	2,268	--
All species	67,688	1,470	3,423	3,304	7,570	7,808	9,265	16,280	5,970	12,597	--
Hickory											
Hickory spp	51	51	--	--	--	--	--	--	--	--	--
Bitternut hickory	9,646	1,065	2,766	1,675	1,692	971	1,237	--	--	--	--
Shagbark hickory	17,342	2,822	2,983	3,265	4,573	3,699	--	--	--	--	--
All species	27,099	3,958	5,769	4,940	6,466	4,670	1,237	--	--	--	--
Yellow birch											
Yellow birch	42,266	4,049	4,366	4,308	3,348	6,162	4,650	6,516	3,904	4,963	--
All species	42,266	4,049	4,366	4,368	3,348	6,162	4,650	6,516	3,904	4,963	--
Hard maple											
Sugar maple	560,780	79,025	113,363	107,591	84,376	54,729	47,518	35,647	12,879	25,652	--
All species	560,780	79,025	113,363	107,591	84,376	54,729	47,518	35,647	12,879	25,652	--
Soft maple											
Red maple	432,610	103,082	123,881	92,114	53,020	25,760	12,932	7,054	5,114	5,941	3,712
Silver maple	128,680	3,224	6,915	7,410	12,863	14,248	13,780	7,732	4,776	32,506	25,226
All species	561,290	106,306	130,796	99,524	65,884	40,008	26,712	14,787	9,890	38,447	28,938
Ash											
White ash	3,253	214	469	1,238	328	--	1,006	--	--	--	--
Black ash	817,880	154,739	205,822	166,724	117,022	75,264	48,302	12,087	10,077	7,002	--
Green ash	305,707	28,006	46,512	49,266	43,676	35,848	30,911	18,137	22,635	27,360	3,151
All species	1,126,840	182,958	252,803	237,228	161,225	111,053	79,213	31,230	32,711	35,868	3,151

(Table 7 continued on next page)

(Table 7 continued)

Species group/ species	All classes	Diameter class (inches at breast height)									
		5.0-6.9	7.0-8.9	9.0-10.9	11.0-12.9	13.0-14.9	15.0-16.9	17.0-18.9	19.0-20.9	21.0-28.9	29.0+
Hardwoods											
Cottonwood and poplar spp.											
Cottonwood and poplar spp.	238	--	--	238	--	--	--	--	--	--	--
Balsam poplar	437,275	74,584	99,881	93,773	73,853	42,987	31,040	9,440	8,518	3,199	--
Eastern cottonwood	102,792	808	1,773	3,716	6,124	5,673	5,342	6,083	4,998	40,942	26,383
Bigtooth aspen	326,806	17,747	32,326	51,672	79,438	58,969	45,857	20,169	10,056	10,572	--
Quaking aspen	3,292,281	407,365	530,012	620,906	602,922	535,066	305,006	167,029	71,114	49,602	3,258
All species	4,159,392	500,505	663,991	770,906	762,336	642,646	388,246	202,720	94,686	104,315	29,641
Basswood											
American basswood	805,897	57,665	106,892	135,782	126,482	121,849	93,024	62,182	44,161	45,504	12,356
All species	805,897	57,665	106,892	135,782	126,482	121,849	93,024	62,182	44,161	45,504	12,356
Black walnut											
Black walnut	30,470	1,223	1,635	4,901	6,138	3,535	7,254	1,055	--	4,730	--
All species	30,470	1,223	1,635	4,901	6,138	3,535	7,254	1,055	--	4,730	--
Other eastern soft hardwoods											
Boxelder	86,340	14,086	18,786	18,923	11,514	10,628	6,120	1,035	3,717	1,531	--
Paper birch	1,158,743	176,674	312,133	294,696	262,653	98,458	52,261	14,721	2,370	4,775	--
Hackberry	17,173	3,638	3,937	4,004	2,642	879	1,269	805	--	--	--
Butternut	10,483	1,169	2,225	3,811	2,119	514	645	--	--	--	--
Black cherry	24,005	4,675	4,928	5,206	2,893	2,398	3,905	--	--	--	--
Black willow	27,676	606	1,473	3,365	3,348	2,561	2,566	2,728	3,036	2,466	5,528
White willow	186	--	--	186	--	--	--	--	--	--	--
Elm spp	48	48	--	--	--	--	--	--	--	--	--
American elm	164,369	34,900	38,760	32,088	22,066	11,077	13,752	3,382	1,056	7,258	--
Siberian elm	3,678	263	191	186	--	1,660	777	--	--	--	--
Slippery elm	33,582	4,188	6,097	6,730	7,526	2,657	508	2,308	--	1,569	--
All species	1,525,670	240,243	390,549	369,196	254,762	130,832	81,803	24,979	10,179	17,598	5,528
Other eastern hard hardwoods											
Sweet birch	352	52	300	--	--	--	--	--	--	--	--
Honeylocust	273	--	--	273	--	--	--	--	--	--	--
Red mulberry	80	80	--	--	--	--	--	--	--	--	--
Black locust	1,389	151	120	--	--	477	641	--	--	--	--
Rock elm	5,906	1,259	1,543	729	767	939	680	--	--	--	--
All species	8,001	1,542	1,963	992	767	1,415	1,320	--	--	--	--
Total hardwoods	10,516,053	1,257,613	1,816,512	1,947,485	1,767,315	1,359,289	926,306	551,792	323,807	493,089	130,845
All species groups	15,272,749	2,295,811	2,934,976	2,798,699	2,271,914	1,746,838	1,174,398	733,547	467,073	687,766	161,734

All table cells without observations in the inventory sample are indicated by --. Table value of 0 indicates that the volume rounds to less than 1 thousand cubic feet. Columns and rows may not add to their totals due to rounding

Table 8. — Net volume of sawtimber on timberland by species group, species, and diameter class, Minnesota, 1999-2003

(In thousand board feet)[1]

Species group/species	All classes	Diameter class (inches at breast height)							
		9.0-10.9	11.0-12.9	13.0-14.9	15.0-16.9	17.0-18.9	19.0-20.9	21.0-28.9	29.0+
Softwoods									
Other yellow pines									
Scotch pine	9,380	5,060	4,300	--	--	--	--	--	--
All species	9,380	5,060	4,300	--	--	--	--	--	--
Eastern white and red pines									
Red pine	3,062,606	641,875	469,671	461,940	381,618	349,147	374,698	367,060	16,436
Eastern white pine	1,650,224	88,851	134,052	135,316	176,403	214,418	236,940	495,689	168,556
All species	4,712,830	730,726	603,722	597,255	558,221	563,565	611,578	862,769	184,992
Jack pine									
Jack pine	1,388,217	519,909	405,234	271,017	123,608	44,016	24,433	--	--
All species	1,388,217	519,909	405,234	271,017	123,608	44,016	24,433	--	--
Spruce and balsam fir									
Balsam fir	1,221,254	637,452	342,634	171,989	59,743	4,014	5,421	--	--
White spruce	1,012,698	249,198	215,339	148,306	162,328	107,567	44,760	85,201	--
Black spruce	861,334	569,996	183,233	54,695	21,123	6,286	--	--	--
All species	3,095,286	1,476,648	747,206	374,990	243,193	117,867	50,181	85,201	--
Other eastern softwoods									
Eastern redcedar	49,700	22,450	17,424	9,825	--	--	--	--	--
Tamarack (native)	1,364,737	635,409	372,415	172,435	88,536	55,632	13,547	26,763	--
Austrian pine	2,134	845	1,289	--	--	--	--	--	--
Northern white-cedar	2,956,818	848,740	714,342	597,477	320,181	219,524	104,674	151,879	--
All species	4,373,389	1,507,444	1,105,471	779,737	408,718	275,156	118,222	178,642	--
Total softwoods	13,579,101	4,239,806	2,865,934	2,023,000	1,333,739	1,000,604	804,414	1,126,612	184,992
Hardwoods									
Select white oaks									
White oak	348,163	--	54,874	63,260	51,826	43,454	32,420	78,146	24,163
Swamp white oak	43,531	--	--	--	2,747	--	11,106	--	29,678
Bur oak	2,161,598	--	404,480	373,353	330,880	321,158	184,144	463,644	83,939
All species	2,553,292	--	459,353	436,634	385,452	364,612	227,670	541,791	137,780
Select red oaks									
Northern red oak	2,829,230	--	470,021	590,288	465,550	374,580	304,069	489,177	135,544
All species	2,829,230	--	470,021	590,288	465,550	374,580	304,069	489,177	135,544
Other red oaks									
Northern pin oak	262,265	--	30,620	32,910	42,611	74,469	29,468	52,207	--
Black oak	17,306	--	1,002	1,782	--	3,081	--	11,441	--
All species	279,591	--	31,622	34,692	42,611	77,550	29,468	63,648	--
Hickory									
Bitternut hickory	16,573	--	7,181	3,960	5,432	--	--	--	--
Shagbark hickory	32,737	--	17,340	15,387	--	--	--	--	--
All species	49,311	--	24,522	19,367	5,432	--	--	--	--
Yellow birch									
Yellow birch	146,544	--	14,895	29,409	22,765	33,014	20,188	26,272	--
All species	146,544	--	14,895	29,409	22,765	33,014	20,188	26,272	--
Hard maple									
Sugar maple	1,192,315	--	354,111	246,178	223,907	172,632	64,060	131,227	--
All species	1,192,315	--	354,111	246,178	223,907	172,632	64,060	131,227	--
Soft maple									
Red maple	500,659	--	216,768	114,612	60,044	34,003	25,328	30,191	19,714
Silver maple	536,770	--	51,177	61,581	62,516	36,370	23,177	164,912	137,038
All species	1,037,429	--	267,945	176,193	122,560	70,373	48,505	195,102	156,751
Ash									
White ash	6,078	--	1,284	--	--	4,794	--	--	--
Black ash	1,246,798	--	510,827	351,100	233,001	59,969	50,872	41,030	--
Green ash	840,595	--	182,721	160,396	143,786	87,041	110,759	136,924	16,968
All species	2,093,471	--	694,832	511,496	376,787	151,804	161,631	170,954	16,968

(Table 8 continued on next page)

(Table 8 continued)

Species group/ species	All classes	Diameter class (inches at breast height)							
		9.0-10.9	11.0-12.9	13.0-14.9	15.0-16.9	17.0-18.9	19.0-20.9	21.0-28.9	29.0+
Hardwoods									
Cottonwood and aspen									
Balsam poplar	755,433	--	311,850	194,565	145,550	45,572	41,899	16,048	--
Eastern cottonwood	468,557	--	22,446	22,872	27,093	26,851	23,124	202,378	143,993
Bigtooth aspen	1,083,930	--	340,026	269,789	218,958	99,238	50,498	54,852	--
Quaking aspen	7,896,873	--	2,573,569	2,439,555	1,443,679	813,820	354,076	254,518	17,656
All species	10,154,193	--	3,247,890	2,926,521	1,835,288	985,450	469,596	527,796	161,651
Basswood									
American basswood	2,355,017	--	539,071	554,670	499,732	362,594	219,506	292,980	66,465
All species	2,355,017	--	539,071	554,670	499,732	362,594	219,506	292,980	66,465
Black walnut									
Black walnut	107,620	--	26,719	16,450	34,945	5,160	--	24,345	--
All species	107,620	--	26,719	16,450	34,945	5,160	--	24,345	--
Other eastern soft hardwoods									
Boxelder	156,840	--	48,804	48,017	28,483	4,971	18,453	8,112	--
Paper birch	1,616,654	--	835,685	435,328	240,636	69,864	11,430	23,912	--
Hackberry	24,172	--	10,725	3,798	5,842	3,807	--	--	--
Butternut	14,904	--	9,293	2,458	3,152	--	--	--	--
Black cherry	41,182	--	12,232	10,768	18,183	--	--	--	--
Black willow	101,737	--	12,216	10,267	11,007	12,138	14,147	11,696	30,266
American elm	251,101	--	86,623	47,118	60,954	15,538	5,002	35,865	--
Siberian elm	10,737	--	--	7,230	3,507	--	--	--	--
Slippery elm	61,738	--	29,868	11,290	2,273	10,663	--	7,713	--
All species	2,279,263	--	1,045,436	576,216	374,034	116,981	49,032	87,297	30,266
Other eastern hard hardwoods									
Black locust	5,085	--	--	2,147	2,938	--	--	--	--
Rock elm	10,182	--	3,053	4,037	3,092	--	--	--	--
All species	15,267	--	3,053	6,185	6,029	--	--	--	--
Total hardwoods	25,062,542	--	7,179,469	6,124,289	4,336,092	2,664,951	1,593,726	2,490,590	705,425
All species groups	38,671,644	4,289,996	10,046,403	8,147,293	5,668,831	3,866,566	2,398,140	3,826,202	890,417

All table cells without observations in the inventory sample are indicated by -- Table value of 0 indicates the volume rounds to less than 1 thousand board feet. Columns and rows may not add to their totals due to rounding.
International 1/4-inch rule.

Table 9. – All live aboveground tree biomass on timberland by owner category,
softwood/hardwood species category, and tree biomass component, Minnesota, 1999-2003

(In dry tons)

Owner category and softwood/hardwood category	All components	Tree biomass component						
		All live 1-5 inch trees	Growing-stock trees			Non-growing-stock trees		
			Total	Boles	Stumps, tops, and limbs	Total	Boles	Stumps, tops, and limbs
Public								
Softwoods	75,424,026	16,010,603	57,544,105	44,053,455	13,490,650	1,869,319	1,413,756	455,563
Hardwoods	139,864,639	20,390,392	108,732,859	78,947,701	29,785,158	10,741,388	8,008,209	2,733,179
Total	215,288,666	36,400,995	166,276,964	123,001,156	43,275,808	12,610,707	9,421,965	3,188,742
Private								
Softwoods	32,726,902	4,995,751	26,885,560	20,890,407	5,995,153	845,592	650,152	195,440
Hardwoods	184,017,807	20,503,213	143,490,530	104,167,160	39,323,370	20,024,064	14,863,669	5,160,396
Total	216,744,709	25,498,963	170,376,090	125,057,567	45,318,522	20,869,656	15,513,820	5,355,836
All ownerships								
Softwoods	108,150,928	21,006,353	84,429,665	64,943,862	19,485,802	2,714,911	2,063,908	651,003
Hardwoods	323,882,446	40,893,605	252,223,389	183,114,861	69,108,528	30,765,452	22,871,877	7,893,575
Total	432,033,374	61,899,959	336,653,053	248,058,723	88,594,330	33,480,363	24,935,785	8,544,577

All table cells without observations in the inventory sample are indicated by --. Table value of 0 indicates the aboveground tree biomass rounds to less than 1 dry ton. Columns and rows may not add to their totals due to rounding.

Table 10. -- Average annual net growth of growing stock on timberland by species group and owner category, Minnesota, 1990 to 1999-2003

(In thousand cubic feet per year)

Species group	All owners	Owner category		
		Public	Private	Unidentified owner
Softwoods				
Other yellow pines	46	- -	46	- -
Eastern white and red pines	38,127	21,615	16,513	- -
Jack pine	7,739	5,400	2,340	- -
Spruce and balsam fir	23,802	12,796	11,006	- -
Other eastern softwoods	34,256	21,093	13,164	- -
Total softwoods	103,971	60,903	43,068	- -
Hardwoods				
Select white oaks	37,134	7,464	29,670	- -
Select red oaks	21,866	6,896	14,970	- -
Other red oaks	3,625	573	3,052	- -
Hickory	405	- -	405	- -
Yellow birch	177	-297	474	- -
Hard maple	15,457	5,799	9,658	- -
Soft maple	30,277	9,474	20,802	- -
Ash	40,245	12,163	28,081	- -
Cottonwood and aspen	101,246	43,075	58,171	- -
Basswood	23,813	8,419	15,394	- -
Black walnut	1,417	- -	1,417	- -
Other eastern soft hardwoods	24,425	1,503	22,923	- -
Other eastern hard hardwoods	225	- -	225	- -
Total hardwoods	300,311	95,070	205,242	- -
All species groups	404,283	155,973	248,310	- -

All table cells without observations in the inventory sample are indicated by -- . Table value of 0 indicates that the volume rounds to less than 1 thousand cubic feet. Columns and rows may not add to their totals due to rounding.

Table 11. -- Average annual removals of growing stock on timberland by species group and owner category, Minnesota, 1990 to 1999-2003

(In thousand cubic feet per year)

Species group	Owner category			
	All owners	Public	Private	Unidentified owner
Softwoods				
Other yellow pines	--	--	--	--
Eastern white and red pines	9,521	5,288	4,233	--
Jack pine	16,955	7,744	9,210	--
Spruce and balsam fir	29,158	20,367	8,791	--
Other eastern softwoods	6,849	5,388	1,461	--
Total softwoods	62,483	38,787	23,696	--
Hardwoods				
Select white oaks	4,951	813	4,137	--
Select red oaks	13,193	2,765	10,428	--
Other red oaks	--	--	--	--
Hickory	168	--	168	--
Yellow birch	86	--	86	--
Hard maple	1,799	835	964	--
Soft maple	3,813	2,503	1,311	--
Ash	7,240	3,161	4,080	--
Cottonwood and aspen	126,002	65,940	60,062	--
Basswood	7,727	1,878	5,849	--
Black walnut	104	--	104	--
Other eastern soft hardwoods	21,307	11,239	10,068	--
Other eastern hard hardwoods	336	--	336	--
Total hardwoods	186,727	89,134	97,593	--
All species groups	249,209	127,921	121,289	--

All table cells without observations in the inventory sample are indicated by --. Table value of 0 indicates that the volume rounds to less than 1 thousand cubic feet. Columns and rows may not add to their totals due to rounding.

Table 12. -- Average annual mortality of growing stock on timberland by species group and owner category, Minnesota, 1990 to 1999 - 2003

(In thousand cubic feet per year)

| Species group | All owners | Owner category | | |
		Public	Private	Unidentified owner
Softwoods				
Eastern white and red pines	5,170	2,687	2,483	--
Jack pine	8,925	3,805	5,120	--
Spruce and balsam fir	56,353	43,054	13,299	--
Other eastern softwoods	11,896	8,155	3,741	--
Total softwoods	82,343	57,701	24,643	--
Hardwoods				
Select white oaks	1,705	547	1,158	--
Select red oaks	5,427	1,518	3,910	--
Other red oaks	663	- -	663	--
Hickory	910	- -	910	--
Yellow birch	554	554	- -	--
Hard maple	3,125	762	2,363	--
Soft maple	5,075	2,781	2,294	--
Ash	5,059	1,866	3,193	--
Cottonwood and aspen	107,662	58,557	49,095	--
Basswood	6,162	3,060	3,102	--
Black walnut	170	- -	170	--
Other eastern soft hardwoods	53,515	28,414	25,101	--
Total hardwoods	190,028	98,068	91,960	--
All species groups	272,372	155,769	116,603	--

All table cells without observations in the inventory sample are indicated by --. Table value of 0 indicates that the volume rounds to less than 1 thousand cubic feet. Columns and rows may not add to their totals due to rounding.

Table 13. -- Detection Survey Results, Minnesota, 2003

Causal agent	Damage type	Acres detected	Trend
Bark beetles	Mortality	1,189	Up by 100%
Hickory bark beetles	Mortality	4	
Spruce budworm	Defoliation	34,601	Down by 60%
Jack pine budworm	Defoliation	18,546	NEW this year
Larch casebearer	Defoliation	1,660	Down by 40%
Forest tent caterpillar	Defoliation	2,254,050	Down by 70%
Two-lined chestnut borer	Mortality	12,557	Similar to last year
White spotted sawyer	Mortality	3,426	NEW this year
Decline (of Scots pine)	Mortality	136	
Oak wilt	Mortality	4,513	
Dutch elm disease	Mortality	74	
Porcupine	Mortality	1	
Domestic animal	Mortality	10	
Flooding	Mortality	7,986	Down by 30%
Wildfire	Mortality	168	
Wind/ tornado	Breakage	586	Down by 75%
Winter injury	Discoloration	17	
Herbicide	Discoloration	12	
Logging damage	Mortality	364	
Unknown:	Defoliation	5,174	
	Discoloration	7,375	
	Dieback	4,155	
Mortality of larch (likely larch beetle)	Mortality	6,079	Down by 50%
Mortality of all other host species	Mortality	11,145	
Total		2,373,828	